EXPLORING
ENERGY SOURCES

Ed Catherall

Wayland

Exploring Science

Exploring Earth in Space
Exploring Electricity
Exploring Energy Sources
Exploring Forces and Structures
Exploring Habitats
Exploring Humans and the Environment
Exploring Information Technology
Exploring Light
Exploring Magnets
Exploring Ourselves
Exploring Plants
Exploring Soil and Rocks
Exploring Sound
Exploring Uses of Energy
Exploring Variety of Life
Exploring Weather

Cover illustrations:
Top H. Verwoerd Dam in South Africa. The dam creates a huge reservoir of water which is used to produce hydroelectric power.
Below left Indian villagers drying cow dung. This will later be used as an inexpensive fuel for fires on which the family's food can be cooked.
Below right A diagram to show the energy released when an atom is split apart.

Frontispiece Inside Murray I Power Station, Snowy Mountain Scheme, New South Wales, Australia.

Editor: Elizabeth Spiers
Series designer: Ross George

First published in 1990 by
Wayland (Publishers) Ltd
61 Western Road, Hove
East Sussex BN3 1JD, England

British Library Cataloguing in Publication Data
Catherall, Ed *1931–*
    Exploring energy sources
    1. Energy sources
    I. Title II. Series
    621.042

HARDBACK ISBN 1–85210–838–X

PAPERBACK ISBN 0–7502–0572–5

Typeset by Nicola Taylor, Wayland
Printed in Italy by G. Canale & C.S.p.A., Turin

Contents

ENERGY IS EVERYWHERE

Energy is essential for life, but it can be difficult to understand. You may be able to see what energy does, but you cannot see the energy itself. However, energy is needed for any kind of action to take place or work to be done. Without energy, no plants, animals or humans would be able to live.

We use energy when we breathe, move or use our bodies in any way. Even when we are asleep, our bodies are using energy to keep warm, breathe and keep our hearts pumping.

We need energy for cooking, providing light and warmth and running cars. We even need it to grow the food we eat and to build our homes.

Energy is present in an unlit torch, a stretched rubber band or a piece of unburnt coal. Although nothing is happening in these objects, energy is there ready to be used. We say that energy is stored ready for action.

Energy stored in the taut string of this archer's bow will make the arrow fly.

ACTIVITY

INVESTIGATING A CANDLE AND MATCHES

YOU NEED

- **a candle fixed in a holder**
- **a box of matches**

WARNING: be careful to keep your clothes and hair away from fire. Get an adult to help you.

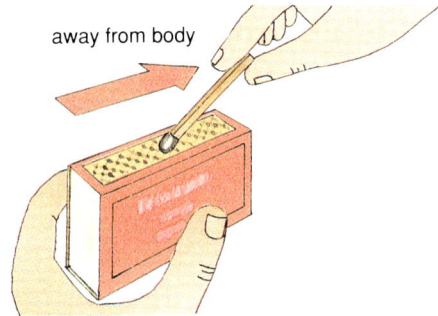

1 Look at the candle and the box of matches. Nothing appears to be happening.

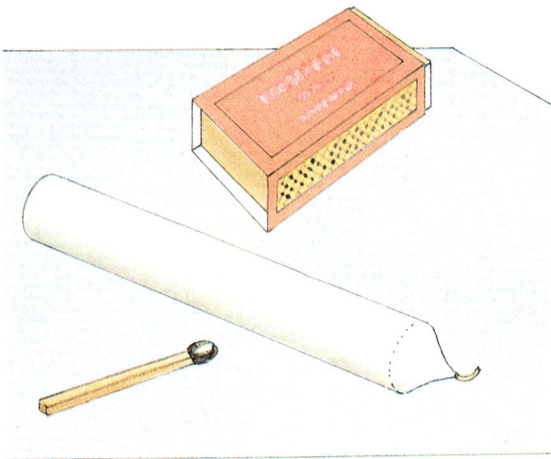

away from body

3 Draw a diagram to show what has happened.

2 Strike the match and light the candle. Your actions have used energy to strike the match on the box and to carry its flame to the candle. The match and candle have burned because they had energy stored in them.

In many homes all over the world, wood is used as a source of energy.

TEST YOURSELF

1. What do all animals need energy for?
2. What sort of things do we need energy for?
3. How can we describe energy that does not seem to be doing anything?

ENERGY IN OUR BODIES

You have already learnt (see page 6) that your body uses energy for every action. When you do something very active, such as running, you might be called energetic. This is because you are using a lot of energy. However, even when you are 'doing nothing' you are using energy to keep your body working.

When our bodies are working, energy is being changed into other forms. If you sit still quietly, your body is changing chemical energy into heat to keep you warm and alive. It is also producing some kinetic (movement) energy to keep your heart beating. If you start to walk, your muscles are changing much more chemical energy into kinetic energy. If you keep on

Even when you are sitting quietly, your body is using energy to think, keep you warm and alive, and in the muscles that keep you supported as you sit.

walking, you may start to feel hot, because a large amount of heat energy is produced. When you speak, chemical energy is changed into kinetic energy and then into sound energy.

Our bodies cannot make this chemical energy from nothing. It must come from somewhere. You may feel hungry shortly after you have been very active, or when you have not eaten for a while. Hunger is your body's way of telling you that you need food so that you can replace the chemical energy you have used.

ACTIVITY

YOU NEED

- **a playground or running track**
- **a tape measure**
- **a timer**
- **a notebook and pen**

1 Measure out 50 m in a straight line.

2 Ask someone to time you running 50 m as fast as you can.
3 Record the time in your notebook.
4 You might be hot, out of breath, or your legs may be aching. Try to record accurately how you feel.
5 Do this a few times.
6 Compare the data you have collected. As you did exercise, your body was using up energy. How did your running times and the way you felt change?

These children are using a great deal of energy as they swim and play. They are changing chemical energy from food into kinetic energy.

TEST YOURSELF

1. What sort of energy does your body use?
2. Which energy transfers take place when you are doing something energetic?
3. How do you replace the energy that your body has used?

THE ENERGY IN FOOD

All animals and humans have to eat food to obtain energy. The food we eat comes from either plants or other animals, which means that all food was once alive. Food, like all materials, is made up of chemical substances. The five main groups of chemicals that our food contains are carbohydrates, fats, proteins, vitamins and minerals. They all contain chemical energy, but the best sources are carbohydrates and fats. The amount of energy in foods is measured in kilojoules (kJ) or kilocalories (kcal).

Carbohydrates are the staple (most regularly eaten) food of most people around the world. In some countries grain crops, such as rice, wheat and millet, are grown as important energy foods. In others, tubers (root vegetables) like potatoes and yams are grown.

Fats are a very concentrated source of energy. This means that there is a lot of energy in a small amount of fat.

Rice is the staple food of many people in the world. These are rice terraces in Bali.

Fats are eaten in meat and animal products, such as lard and butter. Oils are a liquid kind of fat. They can be squeezed from plants like sunflowers and olives, and they are also found in fish such as mackerel and sardines. Although one gram of fat has more energy than one gram of carbohydrate, fats are much more difficult for your body to digest.

All the food that we eat has to be digested before our bodies can use the energy. This means that the food is broken down into chemicals that are small enough to travel in the bloodstream to every cell in your body. Here, the food chemicals that give energy are 'burnt' with oxygen that your body has taken from the air. This is how the energy is released for you to use.

ACTIVITY

YOU NEED

- **packaging from food and drink you have consumed**
- **a diet book listing kilocalories**
- **a calculator**
- **kitchen scales**

What eaten/drunk	Weight (g)	No. of calories
boiled egg		
toast		
butter		
orange juice		
peas		
sausage		
potatoes		

1 List every item that you have eaten or drunk in one day (you will need to have weighed each portion on the kitchen scales).
2 Use your diet book and the packaging from items you have consumed to work out the number of kilocalories in your portions. Ask an adult to help you.
3 Add up your total intake of calories for the day.
4 Compare your intake to the recommended number for your height, build and age. Remember that the recommended intakes are just a guideline.
5 Carry out your survey over a number of days and see how your energy intake varies.

TEST YOURSELF

1. Why do you need food?
2. What are the five kinds of chemical substance in food?
3. Give some examples of the best energy-giving foods that you eat.

PLANTS MAKE FOOD

You have found out that we get our energy from food. All animals and plants need to take in energy. Animals do this by eating, whereas green plants take energy straight from the Sun. They capture the Sun's light energy as it falls on their leaves, and use it to join carbon dioxide gas from the air, and water from the soil, to make their own food. Oxygen is also produced, and is given off into the air. In this way, plants change light energy into stored chemical energy by the process called photosynthesis.

No matter what an animal or human eats, the energy in its food has come from plants. By studying what an animal eats, we can build up a picture of how energy is transferred along a food chain. A simple example of this is when a lion eats a gazelle, which has been eating grass. Food chains often become very complicated, and overlap to make a food web, but they all work in the same way. Plants are eaten by plant eaters (herbivores), which are eaten by meat eaters (carnivores). These in turn may be eaten by other carnivores. In this way food, and the energy stored in it, move up the chain.

Energy becomes weaker, or less concentrated, as it moves up a food chain. Each animal converts some of the food energy into other forms of energy. This leaves less energy stored in the animal to be passed on if it is eaten. This is one of the reasons why the higher up the food chain you look, the fewer of each kind of animal there will be.

Above This green plant makes its food by photosynthesis. It gets the energy to do this from the Sun.

Left This lioness, a carnivore, will get her energy from the herbivore that she has killed. The herbivore has got its energy from eating green plants.

ACTIVITY

DRAWING AN ENERGY PYRAMID

1 Find out about a simple food chain.
2 Draw a large pyramid and mark it into as many stages as you count in your chosen food chain.

Four-stage food chain

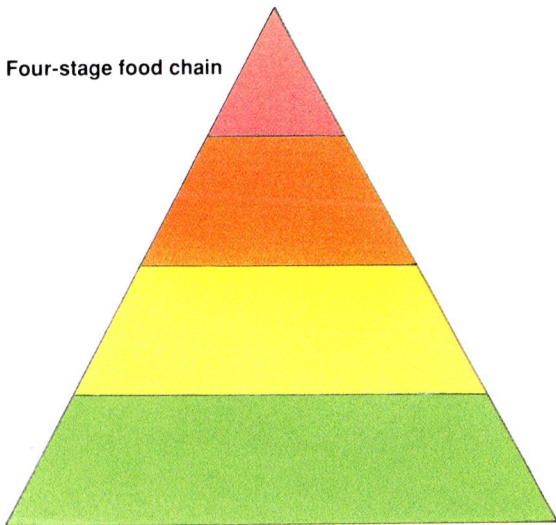

3 Start with the last carnivore in the food chain. Draw one in the top triangle of your pyramid.

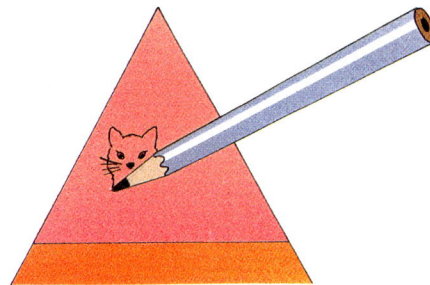

4 Below this, make two drawings of the kind of animal that is eaten by the last carnivore. Carry on drawing more animals as you move down the pyramid.

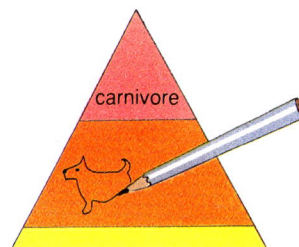

5 When you have drawn in the herbivores, draw the plants that they eat. Show the Sun's rays shining on the plants' leaves. Your pyramid represents your chosen food chain.

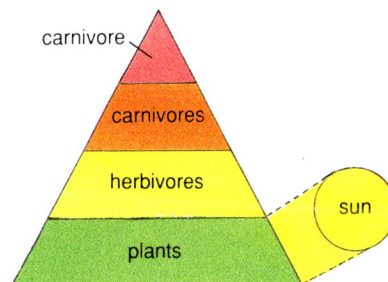

TEST YOURSELF

1. How do animals and plants each obtain their energy?
2. What is the name of the process that green plants use to convert light energy from the Sun into chemical energy?
3. Draw a simple food chain or web.

ALL ENERGY COMES FROM THE SUN

These men are unloading turfs that they have cut from a peat bog. The turfs will be used as fuel once they have dried out.

You know that all the energy in the food we eat comes originally from the Sun (see page 12). In this way, the Sun is the ultimate source of the energy in food. In fact, all fuels or energy sources come from the Sun in some way. To find out why, you must look at the three main areas in which the Sun's energy is found on Earth.

By trapping the energy from sunlight, plants make chemical compounds that store a lot of energy. This process is photosynthesis (see page 12). This energy then becomes available to the whole of Earth's living system, or biosphere. It can be passed on as food or fuel. The fuels from the biosphere include wood, charcoal, alcohol, peat, biogas (gas produced from natural materials) and dried animal dung. The fossil fuels (oil, gas and coal) also store the Sun's energy, because they are made from materials that were once living. They, too, are biosphere fuels:

one of the groups of energy sources.

Every day, the Sun's energy is absorbed (soaked up) by the atmosphere and the water and land surfaces around the Earth. We can harness (capture) the Sun's daily energy in a number of ways. These include solar collectors; wind turbines; wave and tidal power stations; ocean energy converters and hydroelectric dams. You can find out more about these further on in the book. This second group of energy sources is especially important because they are all renewable. This means that they can be used over and over again, as long as the Sun shines.

The third kind of energy that we can make use of is the energy that became stored in the Earth itself when it was formed, hundreds of millions of years ago. When the Earth came together after the 'Big Bang', radioactive atoms were left behind (see page 38). Today, radioactive ore (rock) can be mined from the Earth and processed in a nuclear power station to release heat energy. Heat is also released by the natural decay (breakdown) of radioactive atoms trapped inside the Earth. This keeps the rocks beneath the Earth's surface very hot. This heat can be harnessed by geothermal power stations (see page 42).

Two important sources of energy. The ball is uranium, which is used in nuclear power stations, and the grey material is a piece of coal.

TEST YOURSELF

1. What is the Earth's ultimate source of energy?
2. Describe briefly the three main ways that energy has entered the Earth's systems.
3. List some examples of energy sources that we can use from each of the three groups.

ENERGY IS ALWAYS CHANGING

Different forms of energy can do different kinds of work. You can see, hear and feel some of these forms every day.

Electrical energy flows through cables and wires into equipment and machines such as lamps, televisions, electric cookers and food mixers. It makes them work. The equipment changes the electricity into other forms. For example, a lamp produces light and heat energy, while a television gives sound as well. You feel heat from a cooker and you see the energy of movement (kinetic energy) when food is stirred in a mixer.

Energy that you cannot see, hear or feel is just as important. Some materials, such as wood and petrol, store chemical energy until it is released. This can be done by burning the material, to give heat and light.

If gas or petrol explode, sound and kinetic energy are also released. Food is another chemical energy store (see page 20).

There is another form of stored energy, which is called potential energy. This is the energy stored in an object because of its position. If you climb up a slide and sit at the top, you have potential energy ready to be turned into kinetic energy when you slide down.

Energy exists in many forms and can often be changed from one form to another. We use these forms to power our bodies, and also to power machinery to make our lives easier. However, although we say we 'use' energy, it is never used up and destroyed. It changes and may become spread about, but the total amount of energy stays the same.

In a food mixer, electrical energy is changed into kinetic energy, which turns the beaters. Sound and heat energy are also produced; they are 'wasted' energy.

ACTIVITY

ENERGY CHANGES AND ELECTRICITY

YOU NEED
• **a gift catalogue**
• **scissors**
• **large sheets of paper**
• **paste**
• **marker pens**

1 Work in a group.

2 Take the catalogue and cut out several of the pictures that show items needing electricity to make them work.

3 Work out carefully how the electrical energy is changed in each of them. Remember that many pieces of electrical equipment produce unwanted heat energy.

4 Paste your pictures on to sheets of paper to make a display.

5 Use the marker pens to show how each piece of equipment uses electricity.

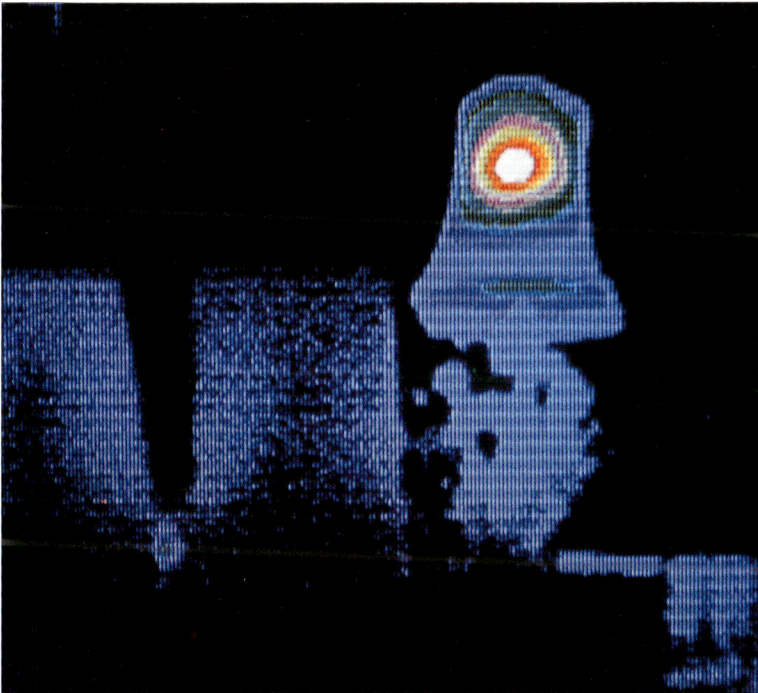

A special photograph of a lit table lamp. Electrical energy is passed through a wire inside the bulb. This energy changes into light and heat. The colour coding shows the hottest parts in white and the coldest in black.

TEST YOURSELF

1. Which are the kinds of energy that you can see, feel and hear?
2. Which are the kinds of energy that are stored?
3. What happens to energy when it is used?

POWER STATIONS AND ELECTRICITY

Left Pylons and cables carry electricity from power stations over long distances.

Below A turbine housing with its water pipe, in the underground machine hall of a power station.

The energy stored in fuels can sometimes be released directly. We do this when we light coal fires or gas cookers in our homes, or run our cars on petrol. However, many of us use energy from an electricity supply.

Most people get their electricity from a grid, which is a system of cables and pylons. The electricity that they carry is generated (produced) by power stations, which are all quite similar in the way they work. They all use generators to change kinetic energy into electrical energy. The generators are driven by windmill-like devices called turbines. Generators work rather like electric motors, only in the opposite way: movement is put in and electricity comes out.

Different kinds of power station use different energy sources to turn the turbines. The heat energy produced by most fuels is used to change water into steam. As the steam rushes along pipes, it pushes against the blades of the turbines and forces them to turn. With some energy sources, it is possible to harness their kinetic energy directly. This happens when the turbines are turned by the force of the wind or the pressure of water rushing through a dam.

ACTIVITY

GENERATING ELECTRICITY

YOU NEED

- **a very large pulley with a handle and a spindle**
- **a 3V or 4.5V motor fitted with a small pulley**
- **Meccano**
- **elastic bands**
- **wire**
- **a bulb holder**
- **a 3.5V bulb**

1 Make a frame from the Meccano.
2 Mount the large pulley and motor side by side on the Meccano frame.

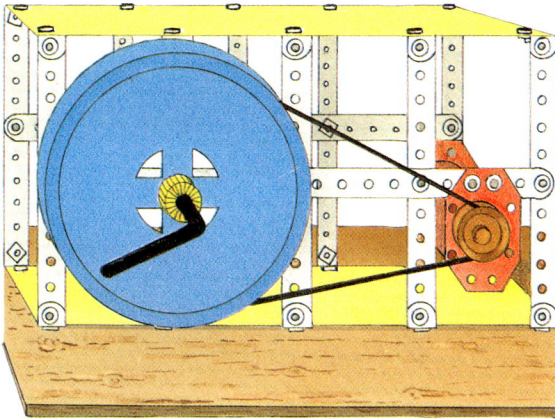

3 Connect the small motor pulley to the large pulley with an elastic band.

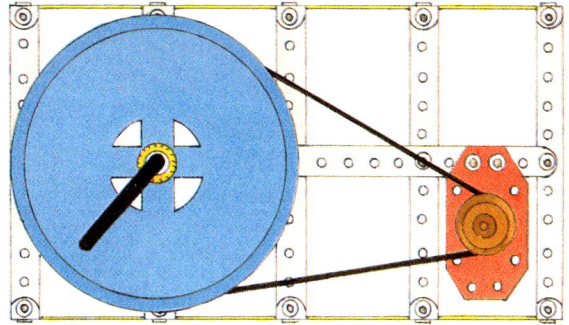

4 Wire the bulb and bulb holder to the motor terminals.

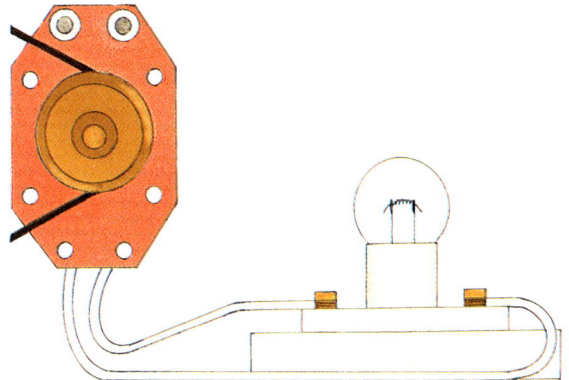

5 Turn the large pulley as fast as you can. What happens?

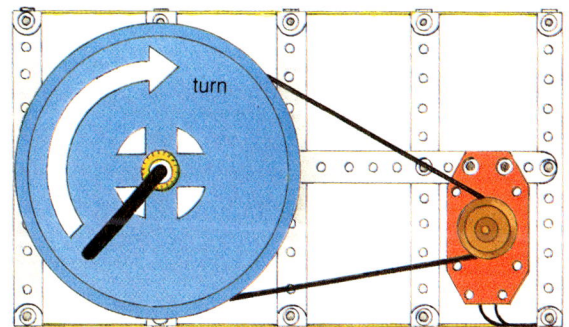

turn

TEST YOURSELF

1. Where is electricity generated and how does it reach our homes?
2. In what way are all power stations similar?
3. Describe the energy transfers that happen with some of the electrical equipment in your home.

STORING ELECTRICAL ENERGY

It is not always easy to plug into an electrical supply, especially if a piece of equipment needs to be carried around. For example, you may want to use a torch when you are camping, or listen to your personal stereo as you walk down the street. Then it is necessary to carry a supply of electrical energy inside the equipment. This energy supply is called a battery, which is a store of chemical energy. When the equipment is switched on, the chemical energy is changed to electricity, which flows through the equipment.

The batteries that we use provide only a small amount of electricity. Much larger amounts can be stored in other ways. A power station often produces more electricity than we need: for example, at night, when most people are asleep and not using most of their electrical equipment. Rather than let this go to waste, the electricity is converted to another form of energy. The most common method is pump storage. Spare electricity is used to pump water from a low reservoir to a high one. As the water moves up, it gains potential energy (see page 16). This can be released as kinetic energy. When more electricity is needed, the water in the high reservoir is allowed to flow back down to the low reservoir. As it rushes down, it passes through turbines and its kinetic energy is used to turn them. They turn the generators to produce electrical energy. This is the way in which hydroelectric power stations work (see page 34).

This person needs to use a torch to read the electricity meter. The torch uses a supply of electrical energy called a battery.

ACTIVITY

INVESTIGATING WATER AND POTENTIAL ENERGY

YOU NEED
- **a funnel**
- **1 m of plastic tubing**
- **a sink or basin**
- **a 1 m rule**
- **sticky tape**

1 Work with a friend.
2 Join the funnel and tubing. Check that the join is watertight.
3 Cover the open end of the tube with your thumb. Hold it 10 cm above the basin in which you will catch the water, pointing upwards.

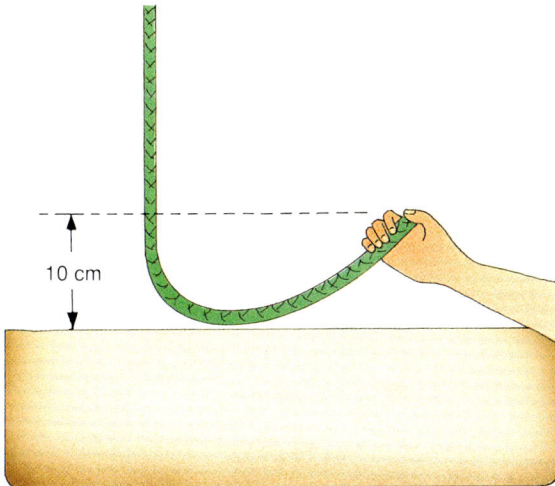

4 Pour water into the funnel until it is nearly full. Hold it as high as you can. Measure and record the height.

5 Remove your thumb from the spout. Record how high the water shoots into the air.

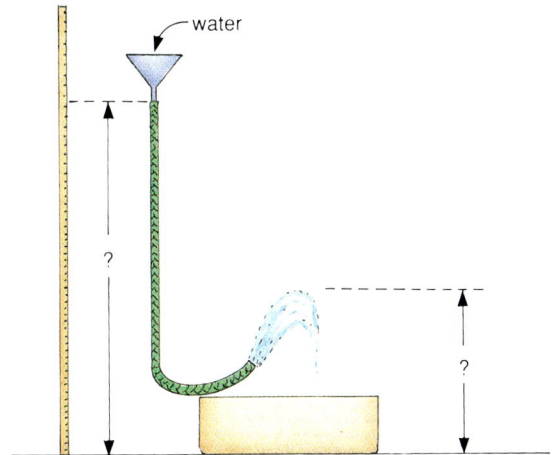

6 Do the experiment several times, holding the funnel lower each time. Record the funnel height against the height of the water shoot.

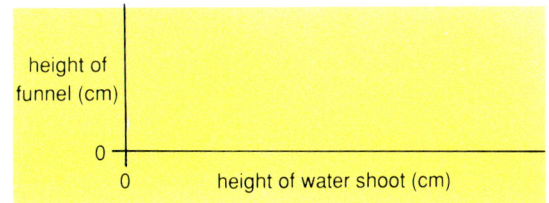

7 Draw a graph of your results. The higher the funnel, the more potential energy there should be.
8 Discuss what the graph shows you about potential energy.

TEST YOURSELF

1. Why are batteries useful?
2. How do power stations store electricity by the pump storage method?

ENERGY FROM LIVING THINGS

Millions of years ago, animals and plants grew and died in great numbers. They were part of the biosphere (see page 14). Some of them have been preserved as the fossil fuels: coal, oil and 'natural' gas. They are used today all over the world as fuel for our power stations, cars and homes.

In many poorer countries, power stations cannot supply all the homes with electricity. The people have to use fuels that they can find near their homes. These fuels come from the biosphere. They may burn wood or charcoal for cooking and warmth.

Waterweed growing on the effluent from a biogas digester in India.

Unfortunately, trees are often used up faster than they are replanted or can grow. In many places, animal dung is collected and dried into brick shapes for burning.

Other fuels from the biosphere are becoming more popular, especially as fossil fuels and forests are gradually being used up. One particularly popular biosphere fuel is biogas. This is methane, which is found in natural gas. You have already found out (see page 12) that animals and plants are energy sources. As dead plant and animal materials decay (rot), they break down into smaller, simpler chemicals. One of these is biogas, which can be collected in a digester as it is

Cow dung has been stuck to this house wall in West Bengal. It is drying out, so that it can be used as fuel.

produced. A digester is a closed container in which the animal and plant remains decay. Bacteria help this to happen, and the process is quite quick because the bacteria produce heat as they digest the material. Biogas is an efficient energy source, because it makes good use of waste material produced in large quantities by living things. Another biosphere fuel is raw alcohol. Some countries grow sugar cane and ferment the sugar to produce very strong alcohol. This can be used as a fuel for special cars.

You know that plants capture the Sun's energy by photosynthesis (see page 12). They pass on that energy to animals and humans as food. Animals and humans release the energy stored in food by respiration. This is similar to the burning of wood, dung, the fossil fuels and any other energy source made from organic compounds (chemicals based on carbon). This means that all the energy captured in the Earth's biosphere by plants is released by the opposite processes of respiration and burning.

TEST YOURSELF

1. What is the Earth's living system called?
2. Make a list of fuels that have come from living things.
3. How are respiration and photosynthesis different?

PEAT AND COAL

When plants die, they usually rot very quickly and become soil. But when plants die in a watery environment, they decay underwater away from air. This slows down the process and the plant material begins to be preserved. In the early stages, a matted soil called peat forms. Sometimes, people cut pieces of it from peat bogs and leave it to dry. It is burnt on fires in homes, and also on a much larger scale in some power stations.

Hundreds of millions of years ago, when the Earth's climate was warmer and wetter, large forests grew. They died and decayed in the swamps and river deltas in which they stood. Over many years, layers of sand and mud built up over the decaying plants. This process happened again and again.

The weight of the layers squashed the material underneath and it turned into a crumbly brown coal called lignite. As the lignite was forced deeper and deeper down, the pressure became greater. This, as well as the great heat below the Earth's surface (see page 39), changed the material from a soft, crumbly texture to a hard, black substance. This is the coal that is mined on every continent of the world.

ACID RAIN

As rainwater falls through the atmosphere, it mixes with carbon dioxide gas and becomes an acid called carbonic acid. This natural acid is so weak that it does not harm the environment.

Left Coalminers at work on the west coast of the USA.

Below A forest and lake in France. Both have been 'killed' by acid rain.

However, when coal is burnt, sulphur and nitrogen in the coal combine with oxygen from the air to give oxides. These mix with rainwater and make it much more acidic. The main acids that this process produces are sulphuric and nitric acids, which are very strong. This acid rain is polluting the environment. It causes trees to stop growing and animals and plants to die in lakes and rivers. It also corrodes buildings, making them crumble.

ACTIVITY

YOU NEED

- **a glass jar**
- **a box of matches**
- **universal indicator paper or solution**

WARNING: take care when using matches. Ask an adult to help you use them.

(shake)

1 Use the indicator to test the pH (acidity) of tap water. A pH of 7 is neutral. Lower than this is acid and higher than this is alkali.
2 Pour a little tap water into a jar and swill it around. Hold the jar on its side, taking care not to tip out any water.
3 Light four matches at once and hold them in the jar as their heads burn. Blow them out and quickly put the lid on the jar to trap the smoke.

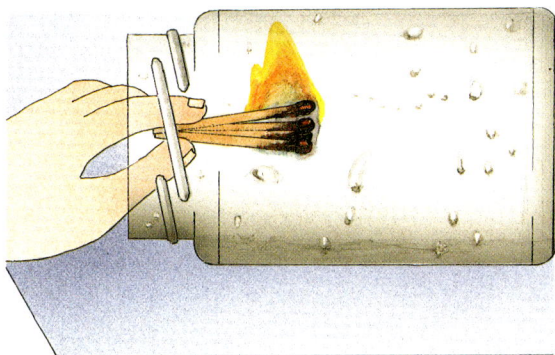

5 Use the indicator to test the water now.

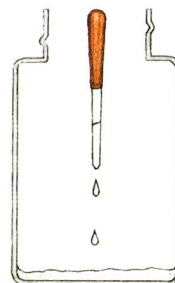

How has the pH of the water changed? When match heads burn, they release oxides of sulphur and phosphorus. These make water more acidic in the same way as when acid rain is formed.
6 You could collect and test samples of rainwater, and compare them with your results for tap water and acid water.

4 Shake the jar to mix the smoke and the water.

OIL AND NATURAL GAS

Like coal, oils and natural gas are fossil fuels that have taken millions of years to form. Animals, as well as plants, died and settled on the sea-bed and became buried. Pressure and heat changed the decaying material into oil. Some of the oil decayed even more and made natural gas. These oil and gas reserves supply us with precious resources that we use today.

Before it can be used, natural gas is purified. Then the methane is ready to be piped directly to homes and factories. Oil that comes directly from wells is called crude oil. This is because it is not just one substance but many, all mixed together. It has to be treated before it can be used. The factory where oil is treated is called a refinery. Crude oil is refined to separate it into products that can be used. These include aircraft fuel, lubricating oil, chemicals from which to make plastics, tar for roads and many others.

Oil can cause huge problems. Leakages and spills from oil tankers can release tonnes of oil into the environment. All sorts of marine (sea) life and birds, are destroyed and beaches are covered in oil. The pollution is very difficult and expensive to clear up properly and safely. The problem is made worse by high winds and rough seas, which break up and spread oil slicks that are already many square kilometres in size.

THE GREENHOUSE EFFECT

When any of the fossil fuels are burnt, carbon dioxide gas is released (see page 25). There is a small amount of carbon dioxide naturally present in the air, but, because fossil fuels are used so much, it is building up in the atmosphere. In these unnatural quantities, carbon dioxide is one of the gases that cause the greenhouse effect.

Gases like carbon dioxide allow the Sun's heat to enter the atmosphere, but stop it escaping back into space. Heat is trapped in a layer around the Earth.

Crude oil is treated to separate it into different products in an oil refinery.

As a result of increased carbon dioxide, temperatures have risen around the world. Greenhouses heat up in a similar way. The glass lets in the Sun's heat, but stops it escaping back out again. In this way, the glass is like the layer of carbon dioxide. Because of this, global warming has become known as the greenhouse effect.

You might think that it would be very pleasant to have a warmer climate, but the effects are thought by scientists to be very serious. Some animals and plants are very sensitive to temperature, and so global warming could cause them to die out. As you know from your study of food chains (see page 12), this could have an efffect on other animals. Also, as the weather gets warmer, the ice-caps at the poles will gradually melt and sea-levels will rise. This will lead to flooding, reducing areas of land and killing off even more living things. It is clear that the greenhouse effect must not be allowed to build up.

ACTIVITY

YOU NEED

- **two glass bowls or tanks**
- **a piece of glass**
- **two thermometers**

1 Place the two tanks next to each other in the sunshine. Put a thermometer in each one and cover one with the piece of glass. Leave them for about an hour.

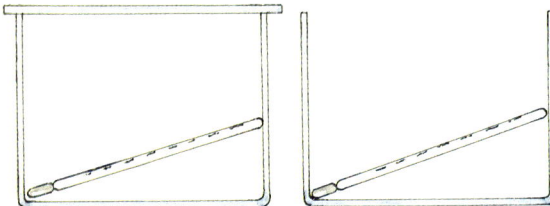

WARNING: take great care when using glass.

2 Record the temperature in each tank. Why is there a difference between the temperatures in the two tanks?

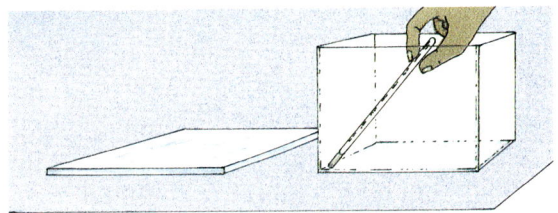

3 Remove the glass lid. Why does the temperature in your mini greenhouse become the same as in the tank that was always open?

TEST YOURSELF

1. What are coal, oil and natural gas made from and why are they called fossil fuels?
2. How does burning coal make acid rain and what does acid rain do?
3. How is the greenhouse effect warming the Earth?

RENEWABLE ENERGY SOURCES

Today, we use so much energy that we depend very heavily on the fossil fuels that have taken nature millions of years to make. It is not surprising that we are using them up faster than they are being formed. There will be a time when the world's limited resources are used up. Because of this, the fossil fuels are known as non-renewable energy sources.

The Sun could be our main energy source of the future.

Every day, vast quantities of the Sun's energy are absorbed by the Earth (see page 15). Even if only a small proportion of this could be harnessed, there would be enough energy for our needs as long as the Sun continues to shine. Energy sources that come from daily sunshine are therefore known as 'renewable'. These include solar power, wind energy, hydroelectricity and energy from the sea. You can find out about them further on in the book. Wood, and methane gas from rotting waste (see page 23), are also thought of as renewable, because they can be formed in a short time in the biosphere.

Many people think that alternatives to fossil fuels should be used more. This is not only because fossil fuels are running out, but because they cause such serious environmental problems. Renewable sources are clean, and most of them are being investigated as alternative energy sources. Some of them are already in use all over the world.

Windmills, such as this one near Gouda in Holland, have been used for energy over thousands of years.

TEST YOURSELF

1. Why are fossil fuels thought of as non-renewable energy sources?
2. What is a renewable energy source?
3. Using wind energy is not a new idea. In the Netherlands, wind-driven machines have been used for many years. What do we call them?

SOLAR POWER

There are ways to capture the Sun's radiation (light and heat energy) directly. These can be used all over the world, but usually work best where the Sun shines most.

Buildings can be designed to absorb (soak up) heat during the day and release it when it is most needed, at night. Usually, the Sun shines through large windows and on to a heat collector, which stores the energy. The heat collectors are usually black, as this is the best colour for absorbing heat. Solar panels on roof-tops work in the same way, but the heat is stored in a liquid such as water or oil. This is used to heat the building by passing it around a central heating system, or simply to provide hot water. The larger the surface area of the panel or heat collector, the more energy it can harness.

The Sun's light energy can be turned into electricity using photovoltaic cells

Above *This special tower in Spain is part of a complex of panels that collect the Sun's rays.*

Left *This solar house in New Mexico, USA, is covered in panels that absorb the Sun's rays to provide heating for the house. Its special shape is designed to give the house strength, while capturing as much sun as possible.*

that contain crystals of silicon. These work in a similar way to a car battery, but, instead of being recharged by something that moves, such as an engine, they are recharged by light. They were first made for spacecraft, but now you may find them powering your calculator or watch.

Solar heat can be captured on a vast scale to generate electricity. The Sun's light is reflected off many mirrors and on to one small target, to concentrate the energy. This means that much more of the Sun's radiation is collected in one place. The intense heat can then turn water into steam to turn a turbine.

ACTIVITY

TESTING SOLAR PANELS

YOU NEED

- **foil baking trays: two large and two small**
- **black paint and a brush**
- **old newspapers**
- **a measuring cylinder**
- **water**
- **cling film**
- **a thermometer**

1 Paint the inside of one small and one large foil tray. Leave them to dry.
2 Lay out all four trays in the Sun, on top of the newspapers.

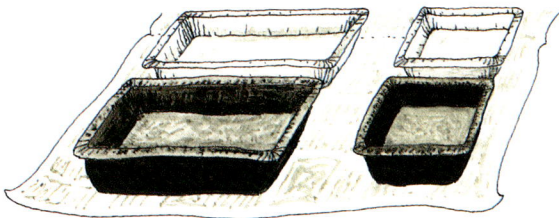

3 Measure 100 ml of water into each tray and cover them with cling film. Leave them for about one hour.

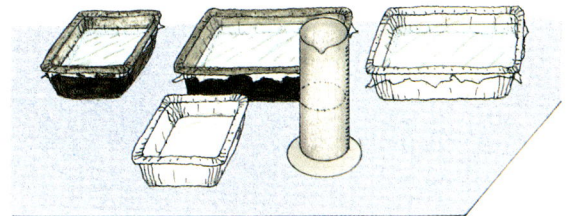

4 Use a thermometer to record the water temperature in each tray, by lifting a corner of the cling film aside.

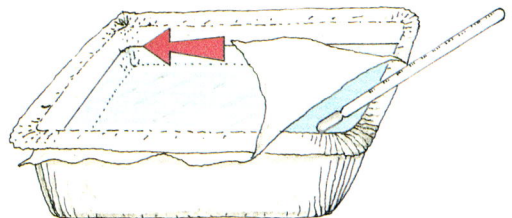

5 Draw a diagram to show the order in which your mini solar panels were best at collecting the Sun's heat. Which is the best design, and why?

TEST YOURSELF

1. Briefly describe three ways that we can harness solar power.
2. If a word has 'photo' at the start of it, what is that word about (think of photographs, photosynthesis)?

WIND POWER

A windfarm is made of a large group of wind turbines, all working together. This windfarm is in the Altamont Pass, USA.

The Sun's energy is mainly responsible for powering the wind systems of the world (see *Exploring Weather* for more information). Wind power has been used for thousands of years to turn windmills. They were used to turn machinery to raise water from deep wells and to grind wheat. In recent years, new ways have been found to capture the wind's energy more efficiently. However, because winds vary from place to place, and from day to day, this can prove to be difficult.

Today's wind turbines are very different from the old windmills. For example, they are designed so that they automatically turn into the wind if its direction changes. However, they can still be damaged in very high winds.

Wind turbines can be used to generate electricity. They can supply the power for a single farm or house, or they may be connected to a grid (see page 18) for general use. To make enough electricity, wind turbines work together in groups as windfarms. In California, USA, one windfarm has 18,000 wind turbines. The problem with large windfarms is that they look ugly and make a lot of noise. It is better to build them out at sea where they will not disturb animals and humans, but this is very expensive.

ACTIVITY

MAKING A WIND TURBINE

YOU NEED

- **two lengths of thin balsa wood, about 50 cm long and 5 cm wide**
- **a large washing-up bottle weighted with sand**
- **a metal knitting needle**
- **a large bead**
- **4 disposable cups**
- **strong glue**
- **sticky tape**
- **a bright marker pen**
- **a timer**

1 Use the knitting needle to make a hole in the middle of both pieces of wood. Glue the wood together in a cross with the holes overlapping.
2 Tape the cups to the arms of the wood. Mark one cup clearly with the pen.

3 Pass the knitting needle through the holes in the wood, the bead and the top of the bottle. Make sure it turns easily.

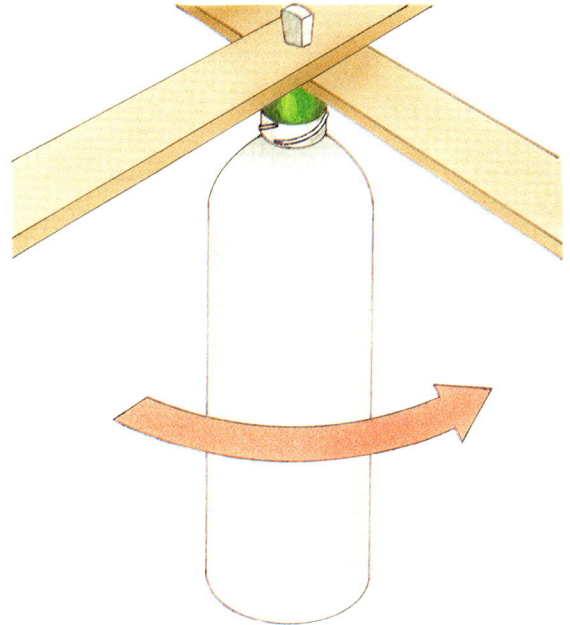

4 On a breezy day, take your wind turbine outside and test it in several places. Try in the middle of the playground, next to a building and under some trees. Record how many times it turns in one minute by watching the marked cup.
5 Try the tests again in the same places on a calm day.
6 Compare all your results. One of the difficulties of wind power is that it is so variable in time and place. Do you think your results show this?

TEST YOURSELF

1. Why is it difficult to harness enough of the wind's power for modern needs?
2. How can windfarms on land cause environmental problems?

HYDROELECTRICITY

Water on the Earth's surface is heated up by the Sun. It turns into a gas called water vapour, which rises into the atmosphere. The further up into the atmosphere you go, the colder it becomes. You know that steam from a kettle turns back into water (condenses) when it reaches a cold area; water vapour in the atmosphere does the same. Tiny water droplets are formed, and eventually make clouds. When rain falls on mountains, it makes gushing rivers. There is an enormous amount of kinetic energy to be harnessed as the water flows downhill to the sea.

Water power has been used for centuries. Nowadays, hydroelectric schemes are used to generate large amounts of electricity. Usually, a dam is built across a river valley, to control the flow of water and store up the energy. The water collects in a reservoir behind the dam. When electricity is needed, the water is allowed to rush through holes in the dam, turning turbines as it flows.

Hydroelectric schemes are used all over the world. They provide a widespread renewable energy source. However, they need to be carefully planned, since they can cause large areas of land to be flooded behind the dam. This can seriously damage the local environment in which plants, animals and humans live.

An aerial view of the Hoover Dam, in Nevada, USA. This is a huge hydroelectric dam.

ACTIVITY

MAKING A WATER TURBINE

YOU NEED

- **a large plastic bottle**
- **two corks, already corkscrewed**
- **a thin metal knitting needle**
- **a sharp knife**
- **running water**

WARNING: be very careful when using the sharp knife. Get an adult to help you.

1 Ask an adult to cut the bottom off the bottle.
2 Cut 4 curved blades from this.

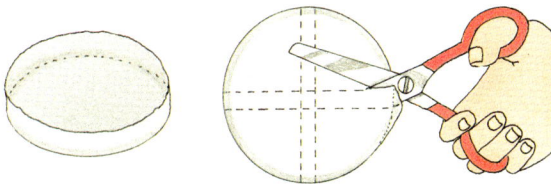

3 Pierce 2 holes halfway down the bottle.

4 Cut 4 slits along one of the corks.
5 Push the blades into the slits in the cork. You have made a turbine.

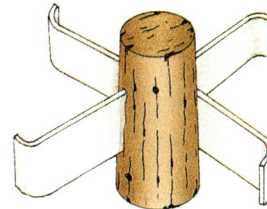

6 Hold your turbine in place inside the bottle. Push the knitting needle into one of the holes in the bottle, through the cork and out of the other hole.
7 Use the second cork to keep your needle in place, but make sure that your turbine turns freely.

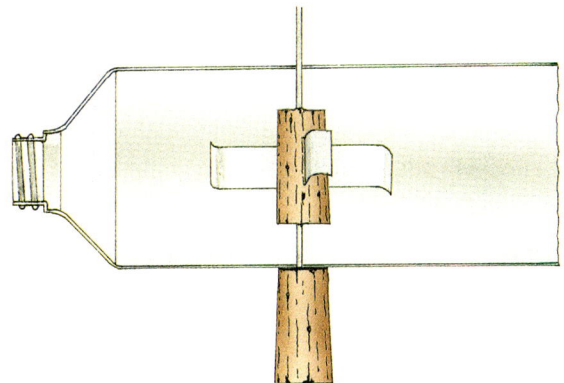

8 Run water on to the blades of your turbine. What happens? If your turbine was connected to a generator, you would be able to make hydroelectricity.

TEST YOURSELF

1. How is the Sun responsible for hydroelectricity?
2. How do hydroelectric schemes store and control the energy in water?

ENERGY FROM THE SEA

The only tidal barrage in the world, at La Rance in France.

There are several ways in which the sea can provide us with energy for generating electricity. Some of these ideas are still being tested and improved.

If you have ever been to the seaside, you will know that waves can be very powerful. Waves happen because winds transfer their energy to the sea's surface as they blow over the water. Wave-power systems use the kinetic energy in the waves to turn turbines. These can be either floating or fixed to the sea-bed, and placed out to sea or on the shoreline.

At the seaside, you may also have noticed that the tide moves up and then down the beach. Tides are mainly caused by forces from the Moon and the Sun. This force is called gravity and it pulls on the water. Tidal energy can

be harnessed by building a barrier right across a river estuary. Electricity is generated in the same way as with a hydroelectric dam, except that it is the push and pull of the tides that causes water to flow over the turbines. However, people fear that tidal schemes may upset estuary environments that are rich in wildlife. Also, tidal barrages (barriers) are a nuisance to shipping.

In tropical oceans, the Sun heats up the surface of the water, so that it is much warmer than the deep-sea water near the ocean bed. The difference in temperature does not even out, because warm water never sinks. Because of this, the warm water near the ocean surface can be used to generate electricity. These schemes are known as Ocean Thermal Energy Converters (OTEC). The heat energy is used to heat up a liquid such as ammonia, which boils to become a vapour, or gas, at a temperature well below the boiling point of water. This vapour is produced very quickly and in large quantities. It can be used, like steam, to turn turbines for generating electricity.

ACTIVITY

TESTING WARM AND COLD WATER

YOU NEED

- **a water tank**
- **dark food colouring, dye or ink**
- **a large jug of hot water**
- **two thermometers**
- **a timer**

1 Ask a friend to help you.
2 Half fill the tank with cold water. Hold a thermometer near the bottom.

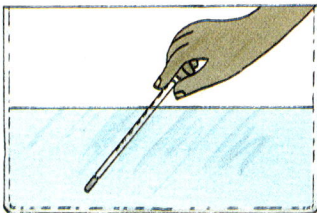

3 Mix some dark colouring with hot water in the jug. Leave it for a few seconds until the water stops moving.

4 Pour the hot water on to the cold, very gently.

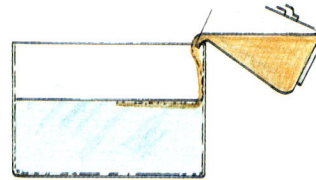

5 Hold the other thermometer near the top of the water. Draw up a table to record both temperatures every 10 seconds and to describe the movement of the colouring in the water.

Time (sec)	Temp at bottom (°C)	Temp at top (°C)	Movement of colouring
0			
10			
20			

6 Ocean thermal energy converters can work because warm water tends to stay above cold. Did you find that for as long as the water was hot, the two layers of water did not mix?

TEST YOURSELF

1. Briefly describe three ways that the sea's energy can be harnessed.
2. What is mainly responsible for causing tides?
3. Why do Ocean Thermal Energy Converters work?

ENERGY FROM THE ATOM

Atoms are so small that you cannot possibly see them. But everything that you can see, or think of, is made up of billions of these tiny particles. Each one of these atoms has a nucleus, or centre. This contains a bundle of even smaller particles called protons and neutrons. There are also tiny electrons travelling around the nucleus. One way of imagining these electrons is to think of them as being like planets travelling around the Sun.

Usually, the protons and neutrons in an atom are held tightly together by energy. But some kinds of substance have atoms that can split apart. When this happens, smaller kinds of atoms are made and the energy held in the original atom is released. Substances that will do this are known as radioactive, and the breakdown of the atom is known as decay.

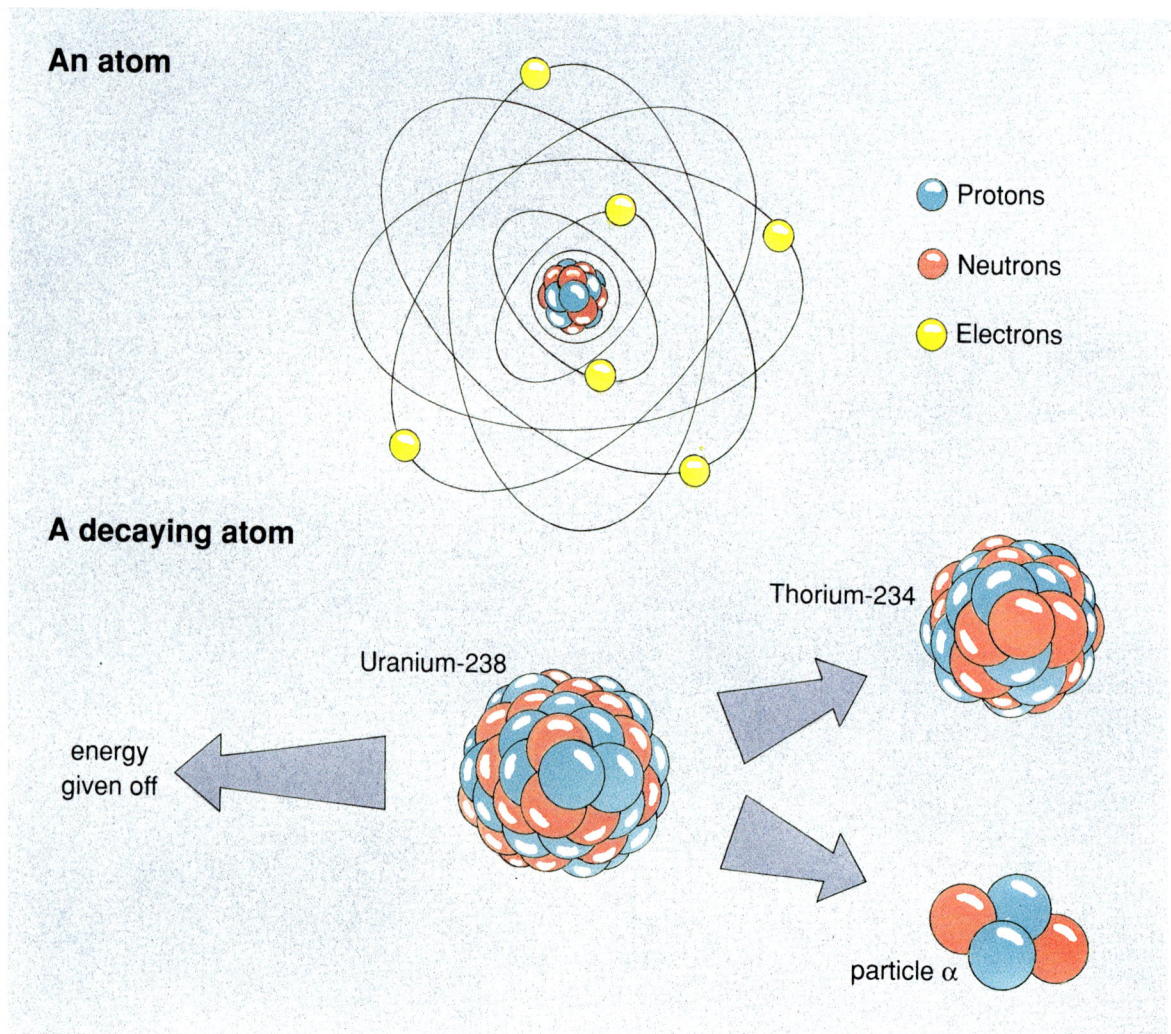

An atom

Protons

Neutrons

Electrons

A decaying atom

Thorium-234

Uranium-238

energy given off

particle α

Radioactive materials remain from the time when the Earth was formed about five billion years ago. We can make use of these radioactive materials today. The radioactive material called uranium is mined from the Earth and is used as an energy source in nuclear power stations. Some of the great heat

Uranium ore is mined for use in nuclear power stations. This power station is at Sellafield in Cumbria, England.

produced by the decay of radioactive materials inside the Earth can be harnessed by geothermal power stations (see page 42).

TEST YOURSELF

1. Everything is made up of tiny particles. What are they?
2. Draw the nucleus of an atom and show what is in it.
3. Describe how radioactive atoms can release energy.

NUCLEAR POWER

Radioactive uranium ore is used to generate nuclear power. It is mined from the ground in countries all over the world. Compared with other fuels, it is a very concentrated energy source, which means that a great deal of energy can be released from quite a small amount.

The energy in uranium cannot be released by burning. Uranium can be split into smaller atoms to obtain the energy (see page 38). This decay process can happen naturally in the ground, but in a nuclear power station it is speeded up in a machine called a reactor. This process is called nuclear fission.

In a nuclear fission reactor, neutrons (see page 38) are fired at the uranium atoms. When a neutron hits a uranium atom, the protons and neutrons in the

Fusion

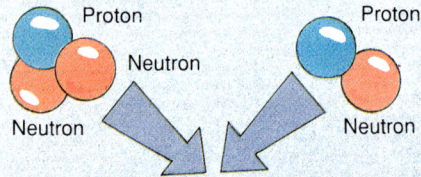
1.

2.

nucleus split apart. More neutrons and a great deal of energy are released, as well as smaller radioactive atoms. The newly released neutrons go on to split yet more atoms apart. In this way, a chain reaction is started. This is a reaction which, once started, can carry on, by itself, producing more reactions of the same type. It can be carefully controlled in the nuclear reactor to give a steady supply of heat. This heat energy is used to heat water to produce steam, which turns turbines.

There are several different types of nuclear reactor in operation around the world. Although it seems to be a very efficient way of producing energy, many people are concerned about the safety of these reactors and the large amounts of dangerous radioactive waste that they produce. Radioactivity can cause cancer, so the waste has to be disposed of well away from living things. One way is to bury it in thick

Fission

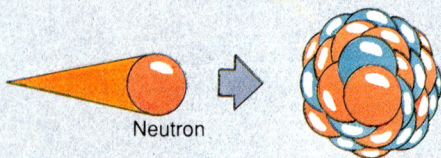
1.

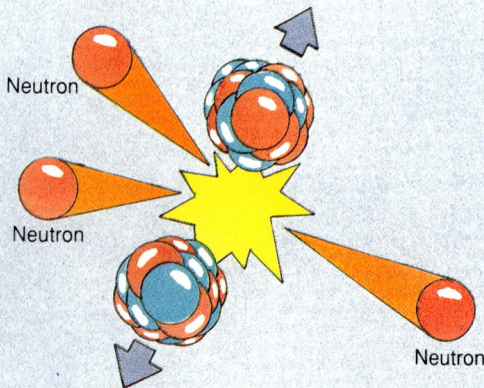
2.

concrete containers. But people fear that these containers could crack apart and release the radioactivity some time in the future.

Scientists are trying to find ways of harnessing the energy from another process called nuclear fusion. This works by smashing together two slightly different atoms, to form yet another type of atom. Vast quantities of energy are produced when this happens, and there are only very small amounts of radioactive fallout (waste products). But it is proving very difficult to produce a nuclear fusion scheme that will work cheaply.

ACTIVITY

SURVEY ON NUCLEAR POWER

> **YOU NEED**
> - **an opportunity to interview people**
> - **a clipboard, pen and paper**

1 Work in a group. Decide on some questions that you would like to ask about nuclear power. Keep the questions simple and try to word them for 'yes' or 'no' answers.
2 Each person should write up the questions in a chart to make recording the answers easy.

Q1		X
Q2		✓
Q3		X
Q4		✓

3 Carry out your survey.
4 Collect all the surveys. Count the 'yes' and 'no' answers to each question and draw a bar graph for each one.

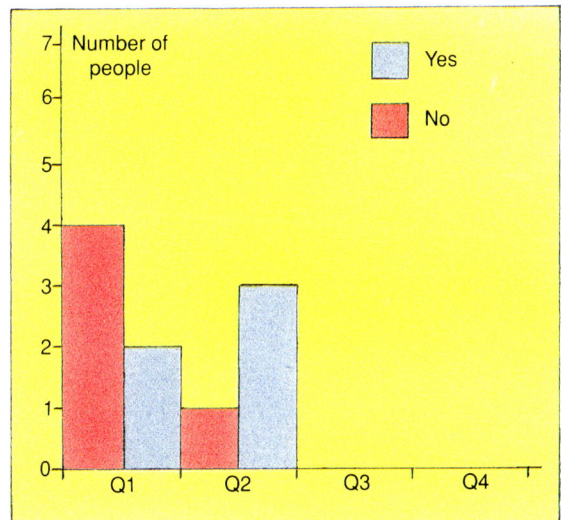

5 Discuss your results. Can you draw any conclusions on what people feel about nuclear power?

TEST YOURSELF

1. What is the name of the radioactive material that is widely mined and used for generation of nuclear power?
2. Briefly describe what happens when nuclear fission takes place.
3. What is a chain reaction?

GEOTHERMAL POWER

You have found out that radioactive materials decay far below the Earth's surface. This releases vast amounts of heat. The rocks deep inside the Earth are kept so hot that they are molten (liquid). Rocks nearer to the surface are not molten but are still hot just a few kilometres down. When water trickles down to these hot rocks, it too becomes hot. If it can find its way quickly back up to the surface, it can be used as an energy source.

There are natural hot springs and geysers on the Earth's surface, in areas where there is volcanic activity. However, some supplies of natural hot water remain underground in layers of rock called aquifers.

Sometimes, there are hot rocks that do not contain water. Geologists are finding ways of drilling down and then injecting water into these hot, dry rocks. The hot water can be used to warm buildings. If it comes out of the ground with a lot of force, it can be used to turn turbines to generate electricity. Geothermal energy is not a renewable source of energy. Aquifers do run out of heat. But there is such a vast supply of heat under the Earth's surface that a new well or aquifer can easily be found.

A geyser in Rotorua, New Zealand. Water is heated by hot rocks underground and is forced through cracks in the Earth's surface.

ACTIVITY

INVESTIGATING HOT ROCKS

YOU NEED

- **a hot radiator or an oven**
- **pebbles or stones**
- **a metal baking tray**
- **a metal tub or bucket**
- **a thermometer**
- **a thick cloth**

1 Put your pebbles or stones on the metal tray. Place it on the radiator or ask an adult to put it in a warm oven. Leave it for about an hour.

2 Half fill the tub with cold water. Record the temperature.

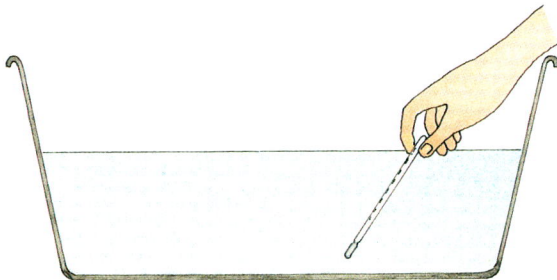

3 Use a cloth to pick up the hot tray and rocks. Drop the rocks into the water.

4 Record the water temperature again. Feel the rocks. Did you find that the heat from the rocks was transferred into the water?

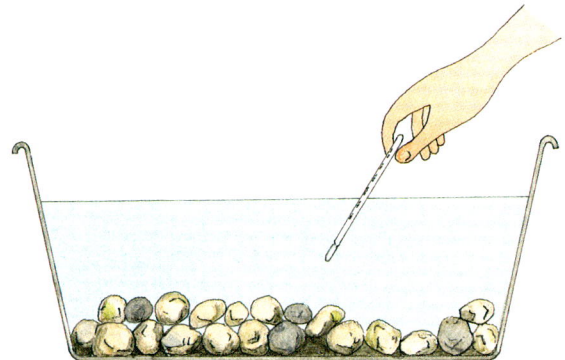

WARNING: if you are using an oven, get an adult to help you.

TEST YOURSELF

1. Why are the rocks below the Earth's surface so hot?
2. How can energy be transferred from hot rocks for our use?

TOMORROW'S ENERGY

In the future, more and more energy is likely to be needed. The number of people in the world is growing rapidly. Each one of these people, especially in the poorer countries, will need more energy if their lifestyles are to improve. At present, fossil fuels supply most of the world's power. But in the future, the use of alternative energy sources will have to grow. This is because the burning of fossil fuels adds to pollution and global warming. Also, the supplies of fossil fuels are running out, and they are more valuable for the production of important chemicals than for heating our homes or fuelling our cars, which can be done in alternative ways.

The use of alternative energy sources will have to be planned carefully as they have their own environmental problems: windfarms create noise; hydro power and schemes at sea change wildlife habitats; harmful radioactivity is produced by nuclear reactors. In addition, in the case of the renewable energy sources, there is the problem that harnessing their energy to supply a steady flow of electricity is very difficult.

In the future, we will have to make better use of the energy that we have. This means using it more efficiently in many ways, so that there is as little wasting of energy as possible. Everybody will have to be involved to make this work. People can insulate their houses to stop heat being lost during winter. Heating equipment, such as boilers and pipes, can also be insulated. Even taking a shallower bath can save energy. Industry can find ways of using energy more efficiently.

In many industrial processes, energy is needlessly wasted: for example, by producing noise and heat. If the machinery were to be more carefully designed, a great deal of this energy could be harnessed. Governments can make policies that help people and industry to be less wasteful of energy. For example, they could advertise on the television, in newspapers and by sending leaflets to each home, telling people how they can save energy. They could give sums of money, called grants, to industry so that scientists and engineers could afford to investigate and build new, energy-efficient machinery. New household equipment could be designed: perhaps to re-use the hot water that people allow to run away, carrying unused heat energy with it. Energy can neither be created nor destroyed, but it can be used more efficiently.

Heat loss in a badly insulated house. White is the hottest area, and blue/green are the coldest.

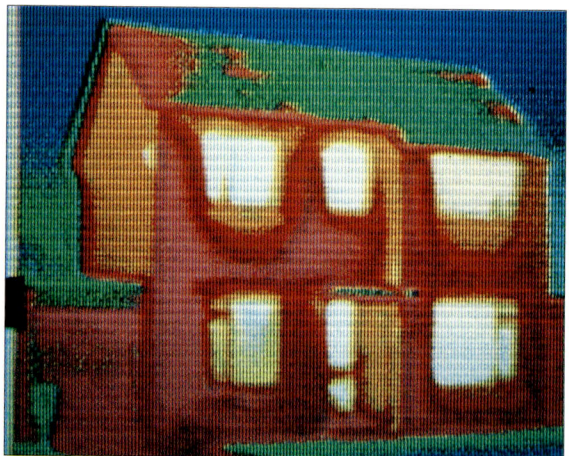

ACTIVITY

TESTING INSULATORS

YOU NEED

- **empty drink cans, all the same size**
- **thermometers**
- **materials to be tested, such as cotton wool, aluminium foil, newspaper, felt, polystyrene beads, foam, feathers, wood chips, straw**
- **sticky tape**
- **hot water**
- **a timer**
- **a notebook and pen**
- **a measuring cylinder**

1 Work in a group.
2 Wrap each can in a different material. Try to make sure that each material is of the same thickness. For loose materials, put them into a polythene bag to contain them and wrap this around the can.

3 Leave one can with no cover. This acts as a control, to show what would normally happen.
4 You can test the cans separately or all at once, but start them all off with hot water at the same temperature.
5 Pour the same amount of water into each can, using the measuring cylinder to help you.

6 Record the temperature of each can at regular intervals: for example, every 30 seconds.
7 Draw graphs, showing the change in temperature through time, for each can.
8 Which materials were better at insulating against heat loss? How did the control can differ? Would you use any of these materials to insulate your home?

TEST YOURSELF

1. Why is there a need to use alternatives to fossil fuels?
2. Why will alternative energy sources have to be carefully planned?
3. In what ways can we use energy more efficiently?

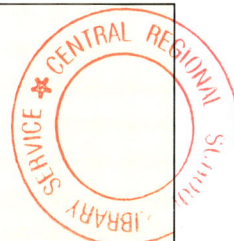

Glossary

Alternative energy   Types of energy used to generate electricity that are better for the environment than using fossil fuels.

Atmosphere   The layer of gases that surrounds the Earth.

Atoms   The tiny particles of which all substances are made.

'Big Bang'   A scientific theory to explain how the Universe was formed.

Carbohydrates   Chemical substances made up of carbon, hydrogen and oxygen. They are energy-giving foods.

Corrode   To 'eat away' at a substance, especially with chemicals. Rusting is a type of corrosion.

Digestion   The dissolving of food in the stomach, to break it down into smaller chemicals that can be used by the body.

Environment   The surroundings of plants, animals and humans. It affects how they live.

Estuary   The wide, tidal mouth of a river.

Fats   Chemical substances found in animals and plants. They are solid and contain carbon, hydrogen and oxygen. They are very high-energy foods.

Ferment   Usually, this means to break down sugars and other carbohydrates into alcohol, using small organisms (living things) called yeast, which digest the substances.

Fossil   The remains of something that was once living, often preserved in a rock.

Fuel   Material from which energy can be released to give heat, usually by burning.

Geologist   A scientist who studies the history and development of the Earth's crust, and the animals and plants that

have lived on it.

Geyser   A spring that spouts hot water into the air.

Kilocalorie   A measurement of the heat- or energy-producing ability of a substance, usually a food. One kilocalorie is about 4.2 kilojoules.

Kilojoule   See kilocalorie.

Minerals   Substances that are not living and never have been. They usually come from rocks and ores, and are found in tiny quantities in foods and water. They are needed by plants and animals to keep them healthy.

Organic substances   Chemicals that are based on carbon, the element vital to life.

Oxides   Chemical substances that contain oxygen and some other element.

Photovoltaic cells   A type of battery in which electricity is produced by light energy.

Proteins   Substances found in the bodies of plants and animals. They contain carbon, hydrogen, oxygen, nitrogen and often sulphur and phosphorus. They are used for growth and repair.

Renewable   Able to be used again, or constantly to make new.

Reservoir   A store, such as a large basin, tank or artificial lake, for water.

Respiration   This term is often used to mean breathing (taking in oxygen), but really means using the oxygen in the cells of the body to burn food substances to give energy. Carbon dioxide gas is the waste product, and is breathed out.

Vitamins   Organic substances that are found in food, and are essential for an animal or human to keep healthy.

Books to read

Energy Book Nigel Dudley (Ladybird, 1981)

Discovering Energy Frank Frazer (Longman, 1982)

Energy Terry Jennings (Oxford University Press, 1985)

Let's Imagine Energy Tom Johnston (Bodley Head, 1986)

Future Sources of Energy Mark Lambert (Wayland, 1986)

Energy Andrew Langley (Wayland, 1985)

Experimenting with Energy Alan Ward (Dryad Press, 1988)

Picture acknowledgements

The author and publishers would like to thank the following for allowing illustrations to be reproduced in this book: J. Allan Cash Ltd, *frontispiece*; Bruce Coleman Ltd cover (top); Eye Ubiquitous 20, 22; Hutchison 23; Science Photo Library 17, 22, 39, 44; Topham 6, 24 (below), 30 (left), 36, 39; Tony Stone Worldwide 34; Wayland 8, 10 (Chris Fairclough), 16, cover (bottom left/Jimmy Holmes); ZEFA 7, 12, 14, 15, 18, 24 (left), 26, 28, 29, 30 (above), 32, 42.

Index

21115060G

TS